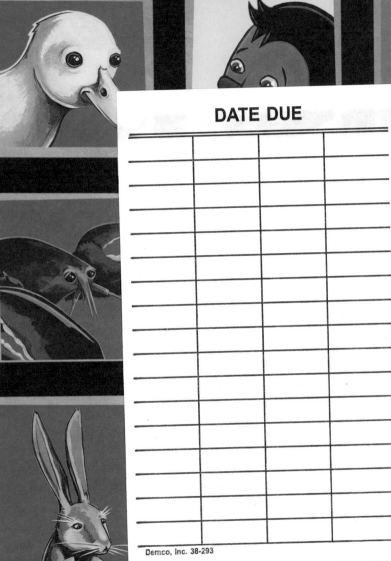

Text © 2009 Etta Kaner
Illustrations © 2009 Jeff Szuc

Kids Can Press acknowledges the financial support of the Government of Ontario, through the Ontario Media Development Corporation's Ontario Book Initiative; the Ontario Arts Council; the Canada Council for the Arts; and the Government of Canada, through the BPIDP, for our publishing activity.

Published in Canada by
Kids Can Press Ltd.
29 Birch Avenue
Toronto, ON M4V 1E2

Published in the U.S. by
Kids Can Press Ltd.
2250 Military Road
Tonawanda, NY 14150

www.kidscanpress.com

The artwork in this book was rendered in acrylic.
The text is set in Bodoni.

Edited by Karen Li
Designed by Marie Bartholomew
Printed and bound in China

This book is smyth sewn casebound.

CM 09 0 9 8 7 6 5 4 3 2 1

Library and Archives Canada Cataloguing in Publication
Kaner, Etta
  Have you ever seen a duck in a raincoat? / Etta Kaner ; Jeff Szuc, illustrator.
(Have you ever seen)
ISBN 978-1-55453-246-9 (bound)
1. Clothing and dress—Juvenile literature. 2. Animals—Juvenile literature.
I. Szuc, Jeff II. Title. III. Series: Kaner, Etta. Have you ever seen.
GT518.K35 2009   j391   C2008-903255-1

Kids Can Press is a CORUS™ Entertainment company

Have You Ever Seen a Duck in a Raincoat?

Written by Etta Kaner · Illustrated by Jeff Szuc

Kids Can Press

Contents

Have you ever seen a duck in a raincoat? 4

Have you ever seen a jackrabbit in shorts? 8

Have you ever seen a whale in a parka? 12

Have you ever seen a cheetah in soccer cleats? 16

Have you ever seen a caribou in boots? 20

Have you ever seen a lobster in a helmet? 24

Have you ever seen an eagle in a baseball cap? 28

Play Animal Tic-Tac-Toe! 32

Have you ever seen
a duck in a raincoat?

4

That's silly.

Ducks don't wear raincoats.
People do.

I wear a raincoat to keep dry. What do ducks do?

Ducks have oil on their outer feathers. They pick up the oil with their beaks from a gland on their backs. Then they spread it all over their bodies while smoothing their feathers.

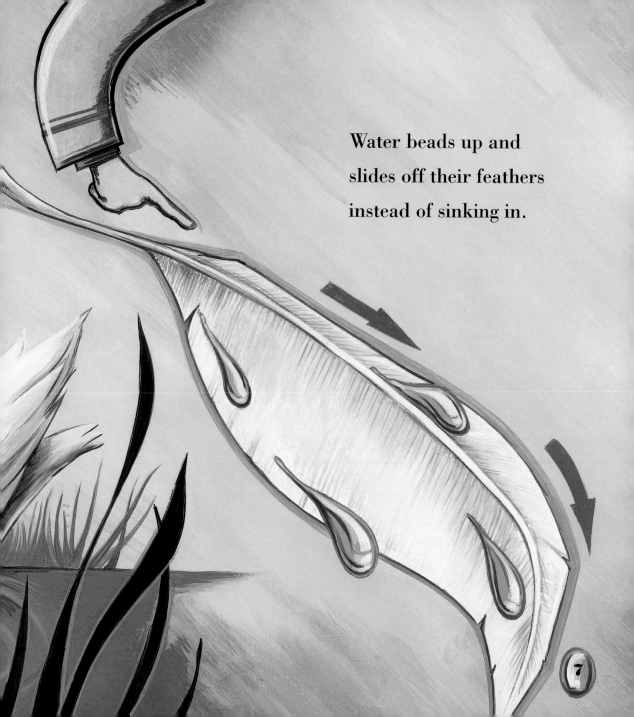

Water beads up and slides off their feathers instead of sinking in.

7

That's silly.
Jackrabbits don't wear shorts.

People do.

9

heat

I wear shorts to keep cool in the summer.

What do jackrabbits do?

Jackrabbits have long, wide ears
that help them cool off in the desert.
Jackrabbits lie in the shade of a bush.
The heat in their huge ears quickly
escapes into the cooler shaded air.
The ears cool off and so does the
rest of the body.

11

Have you ever seen a whale in a parka?

That's silly.
Whales don't wear parkas.

People do.

I wear a parka to keep me warm in winter.

14

What do whales do?

Whales have a layer of fat called blubber under their skin.
It stops heat from leaving their bodies. Some whales have
blubber as thick as the length of your arm. Other whales
have blubber only as thick as the length of your finger,
but it still keeps them warm.

Have you ever seen
a cheetah in soccer cleats?

That's silly.
Cheetahs don't wear
soccer cleats.
People do.

17

I wear soccer cleats to help me run.

What do cheetahs do?

Cheetahs have strong claws that dig into the ground as they run. This helps cheetahs push off and take long strides. Each stride can be as long as four bathtubs laid end to end.

Have you ever seen a caribou in boots?

That's silly.

20

Caribou don't wear boots.
People do.

21

I wear boots to help me walk on ice and snow.

22

What do caribou do?

Caribou have hard hooves with sharp edges. In winter, caribou use their hooves to dig through snow for food and dig into ice when they walk. Hairs on the bottom of the hooves also keep the caribou from slipping.

23

Have you ever seen a lobster
in a helmet?

24

That's silly.
Lobsters don't wear helmets.
People do.

I wear a helmet to protect my head when I tricycle.

26

What do lobsters do?

Lobsters have a hard shell covering their heads and bodies. The shell protects them from predators. Calcium makes the shell strong just like it makes your bones and teeth strong.

Have you ever seen
an eagle in a baseball cap?

That's silly.

Eagles don't wear baseball caps.
People do.

I wear a baseball cap
to shade my eyes from the sun.

What do eagles do?

Eagles have a bony ridge above each eye. The ridge is like a little shelf that shades their eyes from the sun. The shade helps eagles see and track their prey. The bony ridge also protects their eyes.

Play Animal Tic-Tac-Toe!

Have you ever seen an animal play Animal Tic-Tac-Toe? Probably not. But you can play it! Just grab a friend and have some fun.

You will need

- One of the tic-tac-toe grids inside the book covers, or make a photocopy
- 10 counters (such as buttons, checkers or coins), 5 of one color and 5 of another color

1. The first player puts his counter on any square. If his counter is on an animal, he must say one way in which his animal is like a human and one way in which his animal is different from a human. For example: A duck is like a human because they both swim. A duck is different from a human because a duck has wings and a human has arms.

If his counter is on a person, he must say one way in which a human is like his favorite animal and one way in which a human is different from his favorite animal.

2. If the player can't give two comparisons, he must take his counter off the board.

3. The other player puts her counter anywhere on the board and follows the same rules.

4. Players take turns until someone gets three in a row. Good luck!